outdoor plumbing projects

Installing and Maintaining Sprinklers, Pools, and
Other Water Features

harper wells

life level up books, llc.

Outdoor Plumbing Projects: Installing and Maintaining Sprinklers, Pools, and Other Water Features

Disclaimer Notice:

Please note the information contained within this document is for educational and entertainment purposes only. All effort has been executed to present accurate, up to date, reliable, complete information. No warranties of any kind are declared or implied. Readers acknowledge that the author is not engaged in the rendering of legal, financial, medical or professional advice. The content within this book has been derived from various sources. Please consult a licensed professional before attempting any techniques outlined in this book.

contents

introduction to outdoor plumbing projects

. . .

WELCOME TO *OUTDOOR PLUMBING PROJECTS: Installing and Maintaining Sprinklers, Pools, and Other Water Features.* We will walk you through the process of planning, building, and maintaining various outdoor water features such as sprinklers, pools, spas, fountains, and ponds in this book. This thorough book, will equip you to undertake outdoor plumbing chores with ease and experience.

IN TODAY'S FAST-PACED WORLD, it is critical to establish a relaxing and attractive outdoor place where you can rest, entertain, and take in the beauty of nature. A well-designed outdoor space with water components not only improves the aesthetic appeal of your house but also boosts its value. Whether you are a seasoned DIY enthusiast or a novice wishing to improve your outside area, this book provides practical insights, professional guidance, and step-by-step directions to help you reach your objectives.

THE BOOK IS ORGANIZED into 12 chapters, each of which discusses a distinct topic of outdoor plumbing projects. We start with an overview of outdoor plumbing and its significance in building a practical and visually beautiful outdoor living environment. Following that, we go into sprinkler system planning and design, giving you with a solid basis for making educated decisions when purchasing and installing these critical irrigation components.

THE THIRD AND fourth chapters cover sprinkler system installation, maintenance, and troubleshooting. We will walk you through the process of designing your system, choosing the right components, and installing the essential hardware. We will also give troubleshooting techniques and maintenance recommendations to guarantee your sprinkler system runs well for years to come.

. . .

THE FIFTH AND sixth chapters are devoted to designing, planning, and building pools and spas. We will guide you through the process of finding the optimum site for your pool or spa, as well as comprehending the different installation procedures. We do everything from excavation to filling your new pool.

WE WILL LOOK at pool and spa maintenance and troubleshooting in the seventh chapter. We will provide you important information on maintaining water quality, cleaning your pool or spa, and dealing with frequent problems like leaks and pump problems.

OTHER WATER FEATURES, such as fountains and ponds, are covered in chapters eight through ten. We will walk you through the process of choosing the proper water feature for your outdoor space, designing and building it, and maintaining it to guarantee its long-term viability.

FINALLY, in chapter eleven, we go into pond care and troubleshooting in depth. This chapter will provide you with the knowledge you need to keep your pond healthy and beautiful, from water quality management to dealing with algae blooms and repairing leaks.

OUTDOOR PLUMBING IMPROVEMENTS may be both enjoyable and difficult. This book's goal is to provide you the information, skills, and confidence you need to undertake these undertakings with ease. So, let's get started on your adventure to constructing an outdoor refuge for you and your family to enjoy for years to come!

planning and designing sprinkler systems

. . .

A WELL-DESIGNED sprinkler system is vital for keeping your landscape healthy and beautiful. It not only saves you time and effort, but it also conserves water and provides proper plant watering. We will go through the stages involved in planning and building an efficient and functional sprinkler system for your outside space in this chapter.

ASSESS YOUR LANDSCAPE'S DEMANDS: Before you begin building your sprinkler system, you must first understand your landscape's specific needs. Consider the following elements:

- **Climate:** The climate in your area will decide the sort of plants you may grow, the frequency with which you must water them, and the optimum time to water them.
- **Soil type:** The ability of different soil types to retain water varies. Sandy soils, for example, drain water fast, but clay soils hold water longer.
- **Plant kinds and water requirements:** varying plants require varying amounts of water. To achieve effective watering, group plants with comparable water requirements together.

MAKE a basic drawing of your land, noting the placement of your home, driveway, pathways, and other hardscapes. Mark current and planned planting beds, trees, bushes, and grassland spaces. This drawing will be the foundation for creating your sprinkler system.

DETERMINE YOUR WATER SOURCE: Determine the flow rate (gallons per minute) and water pressure (pounds per square inch) of your present water supply. You may need to contact your local water provider for this information, or you may measure it yourself with a flow meter and pressure gauge. These numbers are crucial in establishing the proper size and kind of sprinkler components.

CHOOSE THE RIGHT SPRINKLER PARTS: Based on your landscape's watering requirements, select the appropriate sprinkler heads and nozzles. Sprinkler heads come in a variety of styles, including:

- **Fixed spray heads:** These heads generate a fan-shaped spray pattern and are ideal for small to medium-sized lawns and gardens.
- **Rotary sprinklers:** These heads release a revolving stream of water, covering a greater area and are best suited for big lawns.
- **Bubbler or drip emitters:** These systems, which are ideal for watering individual plants or small garden beds, distribute water directly to the root zone, minimizing water waste.

DIVIDE your landscape into discrete irrigation zones depending on plant kinds, water requirements, and the capacity of your water supply. Each zone should have its own water flow control valve. To guarantee equal watering, avoid combining sprinkler heads with varying precipitation rates in the same zone.

LAY OUT **your sprinkler system as follows:** Plot the placement of the sprinkler heads on your property sketch to get best coverage. When establishing space and arrangement, keep the following variables in mind:

- **Sprinkler head spacing:** Place sprinkler heads around the perimeter of the watering area such that the spray from one head reaches the next (head-to-head coverage). This ensures that the water is distributed evenly.
- **Pipe layout:** Layout your mainline and lateral pipes, adopting the most efficient path and limiting the usage of elbows and fittings.

CALCULATE THE HYDRAULICS: In order to assure peak performance, you must calculate the hydraulics of your sprinkler system, which includes flow rates, pipe diameters, and pressure requirements. This information will assist you in selecting the proper pipes, valves, and other components. You can get help from internet resources or an irrigation specialist.

SELECT AN APPROPRIATE CONTROLLER: Choose an irrigation controller or timer that suits your watering requirements and includes water-saving features such as numerous programs, rain sensors, and weather-based adjustments.

PLAN FOR MAINTENANCE: Include elements such as isolation valves, drain valves, and maintenance access points in your design. Isolation valves enable you to turn off water to certain zones without impacting the entire system, whilst drain valves aid in the winterization of the system to prevent freezing and damage. Access points make it simple to repair or modify your system as needed.

· · ·

COMPLETE YOUR DESIGN: Examine your sprinkler system design to ensure that it satisfies the watering demands of your landscape while also adhering to municipal rules and water conservation recommendations. If you are confused about any part of your design or need assistance in making revisions for best performance, consult with a specialist.

MAKE A MATERIALS LIST: Once your design is finished, make a list of all the materials and components you'll need, such as sprinkler heads, pipes, valves, fittings, and controllers. This list will be useful when acquiring items and installing them.

BY FOLLOWING THESE STEPS, you can plan and construct a sprinkler system that matches the specific needs of your landscape while also encouraging water conservation. With a well-designed system in place, you can keep your outdoor area healthy and thriving while reducing the time and effort necessary for human watering.

installing your sprinkler system

. . .

INSTALLING a sprinkler system is a satisfying do-it-yourself job that will improve the aesthetic and health of your garden. For best performance and water conservation, proper installation is critical. In this chapter, we'll walk you through the process of installing your sprinkler system, making sure you have the right equipment and supplies and offering step-by-step directions to help you succeed.

GATHER TOOLS AND MATERIALS: Before you begin the installation procedure, gather all of the tools and materials listed in Chapter 2's design and materials list. The following are some of the necessary tools:

- **Trenching shovel or trencher**
- **Pipe cutter or hacksaw**
- **Pipe wrench**
- **PVC primer and cement**
- **Teflon tape**
- **Pipe clamps and fittings**
- **Sprinkler heads and nozzles**
- **Irrigation controller**
- **Wiring and wire connectors**

OBTAIN the appropriate permissions and identify utilities: Check with your local building department to determine if any permits are necessary for the installation of your sprinkler system. In addition, contact your local utility providers to have underground utility lines designated to avoid any damage during the installation procedure.

SET UP THE SITE: Clear the installation area of any rubbish or objects that might obstruct the installation procedure. indicate the trench lines using spray paint or string and indicate the placement of the sprinkler heads, valves, and pipes according on your plan.

. . .

DIG TRENCHES: Dig trenches following the specified lines with a trenching shovel or rent a trencher. The trench depth will be determined by the type of pipes used and the frost line in your location. Trenches should be 6 to 12 inches deep in general to protect pipes from freezing and damage. If drip irrigation is part of your design, you may need to dig shallow holes or use landscaping staples to anchor the tubing to the ground.

INSTALL the main cutoff valve and the backflow preventer: To manage the water supply to your sprinkler system, install a main shutoff valve near the water source. For maintenance and emergency cutoff, this valve should be conveniently accessible. Install a backflow preventer as well to keep polluted water from entering your home's water supply. Most municipal construction rules include backflow preventers, which are critical for securing your water supply.

LAY OUT AND CONNECT PIPES: Begin by laying out the mainline and lateral pipes in the trenches according to your plan. To join PVC pipes and fittings, use PVC primer and cement to ensure that they are well seated and secure. To make watertight connections with polyethylene pipes, utilize barbed fittings and pipe clamps.

INSTALL SPRINKLER HEADS AND NOZZLES: Install the sprinkler heads at the required places, using appropriate risers or swing joints to link them to the lateral pipes. To avoid damage while mowing, adjust the sprinkler heads' height so that they are flush with or slightly above the ground. Attach the necessary nozzles to the sprinkler heads, making sure they are properly orientated for best coverage.

INSTALL VALVES AND VALVE BOXES: Place the valves for each irrigation zone in valve boxes, which are protective enclosures that safeguard the valves and allow for simple access during maintenance. Using the necessary fittings and pipe cement, connect the valves to the mainline and lateral pipes. Follow the manufacturer's instructions and local electrical rules when wiring the valves to the irrigation controller.

INSTALL the irrigation controller as follows: Install the irrigation controller in a convenient and weather-protected position, such as inside a weatherproof enclosure. Follow the manufacturer's instructions and local electrical rules when connecting the controller to the valves and power supply. Program the controller to meet your landscape's watering requirements and schedule, taking into account plant varieties, soil conditions, and climate.

BEFORE FINISHING THE INSTALLATION, flush the system to eliminate any debris that may have entered the pipes during the installation procedure. To do so, remove the nozzles from the sprinkler heads temporarily, open the main cutoff valve, and turn on each zone one at a time. Allow a few minutes for water to run through the pipes and out the open sprinkler heads before turning off the zone and replacing the nozzles.

BACKFILL TRENCHES and adjust sprinkler heads: Backfill the trenches carefully with earth, being careful not to damage the pipes or sprinkler heads. To reduce settling, compact the soil surrounding the pipes. Make any necessary adjustments to the sprinkler heads to ensure optimum alignment and coverage.

. . .

RUN the system through its paces: To guarantee correct functioning, turn on the irrigation controller and operate each zone one at a time. Examine the sprinkler heads, nozzles, and controller settings for leaks and make any required modifications to ensure consistent and effective watering. Make a list of any concerns that require more attention or modifications.

FINISH AND CLEAN UP: Once you're pleased with the system's performance, fill in any residual soil depressions, reseed any damaged grass patches, and clean up any installation debris.

YOU CAN EFFECTIVELY INSTALL a sprinkler system that will keep your landscape healthy and beautiful while conserving water and minimizing the time and effort necessary for hand watering by following these instructions. Remember to maintain your system on a regular basis, as described in Chapter 4, to guarantee its sustained efficiency and lifespan. You may enjoy the benefits of a healthy outdoor environment and higher home value with a well-installed and maintained sprinkler system.

maintaining and troubleshooting sprinklers

· · ·

A WELL-MAINTAINED sprinkler system ensures that the appropriate amount of water is applied to your landscape, encourages water conservation, and extends the life of your irrigation components. This chapter will go over basic maintenance activities as well as troubleshooting tips for typical sprinkler system difficulties.

INSPECTIONS ON A REGULAR BASIS: Inspect your sprinkler system on a regular basis for signs of damage, leaks, or malfunctioning components. Examine the sprinkler heads for broken or misaligned parts, blocked nozzles, and leaks in the pipes or valves. To ensure optimal operation, make any necessary repairs or modifications.

NOZZLES SHOULD BE CLEANED and replaced on a regular basis since they can become clogged with dirt and debris over time, impacting the spray pattern and water distribution. Clean the nozzles with a tiny brush or toothpick on a regular basis to eliminate any clogs. Replace a damaged or overly worn nozzle with a new one of the same type and size.

SPRINKLER HEAD ALIGNMENT and spray pattern should be checked on a regular basis to ensure even water coverage. Adjust the spray's arc, radius, or trajectory as needed to maximize coverage and avoid overwatering or underwatering. Raise or lower sprinkler heads as needed to keep them at the right height above the ground.

EXAMINE and modify the irrigation schedule: Throughout the year, keep an eye on your landscape's water requirements and alter your irrigation schedule accordingly. Watering frequency, duration, and start timings may need to be adjusted due to changing weather conditions, plant development, and seasonal changes. For best water conservation, use a smart irrigation controller with weather-based adjustments.

INSPECT AND CLEAN FILTERS: To defend against dirt and silt, many sprinkler systems have filters placed at various places such as the mainline, valves, or sprinkler heads. Inspect and clean these filters on a regular basis to guarantee adequate water flow and prevent blockage.

BACKFLOW PREVENTERS ARE REQUIRED by most local building requirements and are used to protect your home's water supply from contamination. Test your backflow preventer once a year and perform any necessary maintenance, such as cleaning or replacing parts, to ensure optimal operation.

WINTERIZE YOUR SYSTEM: In areas where temperatures fall below freezing, winterizing your sprinkler system is critical to preventing damage from freezing and expanding water. Drain the water from the pipes, valves, and sprinkler heads and turn off the system's water supply. Use an air compressor to remove any residual water from the pipes. If your irrigation controller is not suited for outside use in cold temperatures, make sure to disconnect it and store it indoors.

Common Sprinkler System Troubleshooting

CHECK FOR LEAKS, clogged nozzles, or partially closed valves if you notice low water pressure in one or more zones. Clean or replace clogged nozzles and repair any leaks. If the problem persists, engage a specialist to examine the hydraulics of the system and make any necessary adjustments.

SPRINKLER HEADS **that do not pop up:** If one or more sprinkler heads do not pop up while the system is running, look for debris or dirt that is impeding the sprinkler head's movement. Remove any impediments from the area around the sprinkler head. If the problem persists, the sprinkler head may have been damaged and will need to be replaced.

. . .

INCONSISTENT SPRAY PATTERNS can be caused by clogged nozzles, worn or damaged sprinkler heads, or misplaced heads. Clogged nozzles should be cleaned or replaced, and damaged sprinkler heads should be replaced. Adjust the heads' alignment to ensure optimum spray coverage.

LEAKS CAN HAPPEN at sprinkler heads, valves, or even in the pipelines themselves. Examine the system for signs of water pooling or damp spots in your landscape, which could indicate a leak. Repair or replace any damaged components, and if necessary, seek professional assistance in locating and repairing leaks in subterranean pipes.

CHECK the irrigation controller for appropriate programming and confirm that the valve wires are firmly connected if a specific zone does not turn on. Examine the valve for any debris or damage that is preventing it from opening. If the problem persists, the valve may be defective and must be replaced.

IF YOUR IRRIGATION controller is not working, first ensure that it is powered on and that the wiring connections are secure. Examine the fuse or circuit breaker and, if necessary, replace it. If the problem persists, refer to the manufacturer's troubleshooting instructions or contact customer service.

OVERWATERING or underwatering can occur as a result of inappropriate controller settings, faulty sprinkler heads or valves, or poor system design. Examine your watering schedule and make any adjustments based on the needs of your landscape. Repair or replace any faulty components, and if necessary, call a professional to examine and adapt the design of your system for efficient watering.

WATER HAMMER IS a loud noise created by an abrupt shift in water flow that can damage pipes and components. Install water hammer arresters or pressure regulators at the mainline to prevent water hammer, and make sure valves open and close gently. If the problem persists, get professional help for an assessment and recommendations.

YOU CAN PRESERVE the longevity and effectiveness of your irrigation system by performing regular maintenance on it and resolving typical concerns as soon as they arise. A well-maintained sprinkler system will help you save water, save time and effort on manual watering, and keep your landscape healthy and beautiful.

designing and planning your pool or spa

. . .

A SWIMMING POOL or spa can be an excellent addition to your home, providing hours of relaxation, amusement, and exercise. The size, form, materials, and features that will best suit your needs and tastes must all be carefully considered when designing and planning your pool or spa. In this chapter, we will go over crucial steps in the design and planning process to assist you in creating the ideal pool or spa for your outdoor environment.

DETERMINE YOUR PURPOSE AND OBJECTIVES: Before beginning the design process, you must first determine the primary purpose of your pool or spa. Will it primarily serve the purpose of relaxation, fitness, or entertainment? Your objectives will determine the size, design, and features of your pool or spa, as well as the overall project price.

DETERMINE the maximum size for your pool or spa by measuring and evaluating the available space in your yard. Consider property lines, setbacks, and easements, as well as your home's and other structures' proximity. Remember to include extra features like decking, landscaping, and fencing in your space layout.

INVESTIGATE LOCAL REGULATIONS AND PERMITS: Learn about local building standards and regulations pertaining to pools and spas, such as fence, safety features, and setbacks. To minimize delays and potential fines, obtain the essential licenses before beginning work.

SELECT THE TYPE AND MATERIALS: In-ground, aboveground, and portable pools and spas are all available. Each variety has advantages and disadvantages, as well as cost and installation complexity differences.

Consider the pool or spa structural materials you want, such as concrete, fiberglass, or vinyl liner. The materials you choose will have an impact on the appearance, durability, and maintenance requirements of your pool or spa.

WHEN CHOOSING the material for your pool, it's essential to weigh the pros and cons of each option to find the best fit for your needs, budget, and aesthetic preferences. The main types of pool materials include concrete, fiberglass, and vinyl liner pools. Below is a list of pros and cons for each of these materials:

Concrete Pools

PROS:

1. **Highly customizable:** Concrete pools can be built in any size, shape, and depth, allowing for unique designs and features.
2. **Durable:** Concrete pools are robust and long-lasting, with a lifespan of several decades when properly maintained.
3. **Aesthetic appeal:** Concrete pools can be finished with various materials, such as

plaster, tile, or aggregate, for a high-end, luxurious appearance.

Cons:

1. **Higher installation cost:** Concrete pools are typically the most expensive to install compared to other materials.
2. **Longer installation time:** Due to the construction process, concrete pools can take several months to complete.
3. **Higher maintenance:** Concrete pools require more frequent maintenance, including acid washing and resurfacing, to maintain their appearance and structural integrity.

Fiberglass Pools

PROS:

1. **Quick installation:** Fiberglass pools are pre-manufactured shells, which can be installed in a matter of weeks.

2. **Low maintenance:** The smooth, non-porous surface of fiberglass pools requires less cleaning and fewer chemicals to maintain water quality.
3. **Energy-efficient:** Fiberglass pools have better insulation properties than concrete pools, potentially reducing heating costs.

Cons:

1. **Limited customization:** Fiberglass pools come in pre-made shapes and sizes, offering less flexibility in design compared to concrete pools.
2. **Transportation and access:** Fiberglass pool shells can be large and may require special transportation and access to your property.
3. **Potential for repairs:** While fiberglass pools are durable, they can be susceptible to cracks or damage from ground movement or extreme temperatures.

Vinyl Liner Pools

PROS:

1. Lower initial cost: Vinyl liner pools are typically the most affordable option for pool installation.
2. Customizable: Vinyl liner pools can be built in various shapes and sizes, offering a degree of customization.
3. Smooth surface: The vinyl liner provides a smooth, non-abrasive surface, making it comfortable for swimmers.

Cons:

1. **Shorter lifespan:** Vinyl liners have a shorter lifespan compared to concrete or fiberglass, usually needing replacement every 7-15 years.
2. **Maintenance:** Vinyl liners can be prone to punctures or tears, requiring patching or replacement.
3. **Limited aesthetic options:** Vinyl liner pools have fewer finish options compared to concrete pools, which could affect the overall appearance.

CHOOSE A SHAPE AND DESIGN: Your pool or spa's shape and design should compliment your landscape and architectural style, as well as fit within the available area. Rectangular, kidney, freeform, and geometric pool shapes are popular, while spas can be round, square, or custom-shaped. For increased practicality and visual appeal, consider including features such as steps, benches, or a beach entry.

PLAN FOR CIRCULATION AND FILTRATION: A correctly constructed circulation and filtration system is critical for keeping your pool or spa clean and clear. Based on the size, usage, and local water quality of your pool or spa, select the proper size and kind of pump, filter, and sanitizer. If you need help choosing the proper equipment, see an expert.

CONSIDER ADDING FEATURES AND FACILITIES: Enhance your pool or spa experience by adding features and amenities like waterfalls, fountains, slides, or jets. Other alternatives for extending your swimming season include LED lighting, automatic pool covers, and heating systems. When selecting additional features, keep your budget in mind, as these can drastically increase the final project cost.

. . .

MAKE A SAFETY AND ACCESSIBILITY PLAN: To prevent unwanted access and accidents, include safety features such as fences, alarms, and self-closing gates. Consider accessibility features such as ramps, handrails, and lifts for people with mobility issues.

CREATE A BUDGET: Create a budget for your pool or spa project, taking into account construction, landscaping, and extra features. Keep in mind that continuing maintenance and operational costs, such as utilities, chemicals, and repairs, must be considered. Prepare for cost overruns or unexpected charges that may occur during the construction process.

HIRE A PROFESSIONAL CONTRACTOR: Unless you have substantial experience in pool or spa construction, hiring a professional contractor to supervise the job is strongly suggested. Look for a contractor with a good reputation, sufficient licensing and insurance, and a portfolio of past work that matches your design tastes. Request many quotations and compare them to ensure you are getting the most value for your money.

. . .

PLAN FOR LANDSCAPING AND HARDSCAPING: The area around your pool or spa should be carefully designed to compliment the overall appearance and offer a smooth transition between the pool or spa and your outside space. Consider slip-resistant and long-lasting materials for decking, patios, and walks. Plants, trees, and privacy screens are examples of landscaping components that can be used to create an inviting and soothing environment.

PLAN THE BUILDING TIMELINE: Develop a construction timeline with your contractor, taking into account elements such as permit approvals, weather conditions, and any delays. Allow for timetable flexibility because unexpected obstacles may develop during the construction process.

YOU MAY BUILD a beautiful and functional addition to your outdoor space that matches your needs and tastes by following these steps and carefully examining the various aspects of designing and planning your pool or spa. To guarantee the greatest potential conclusion for your project, engage with professionals as needed along the process. Once done, you will be able to enjoy the numerous advantages of having a pool or spa in your backyard, such as relaxation, entertainment, and enhanced property value.

pool and spa installation

· · ·

THE INSTALLATION PROCEDURE is what comes next once the design and planning stages of your pool or spa are complete. Your pool or spa's long-term usability, toughness, and safety depend on proper installation. The crucial procedures and factors for a successful pool or spa installation will be covered in this chapter.

USE A REPUTED CONTRACTOR: As noted in the previous chapter, it is strongly advised that you use a competent contractor with installation expertise for pools and spas. A reliable contractor will have the skills, tools, and resources required to guarantee a flawless installation. Before choosing the best contractor for your job, do some local contractor research, read reviews, and request many bids.

OBTAIN INSPECTIONS AND PERMITS: Before starting any construction, be sure you have obtained all inspections and permits necessary to comply with local building codes. Permits for electrical, plumbing, and structural work as well as inspections carried out during the building process may be included. Inadequate permissions might lead to penalties, holdups, and perhaps legal problems.

SITE PREPARATION: Setting up the building site is the first stage in the installation procedure. This might entail leveling the ground, removing any trees or other obstructions, and delineating the pool or spa's limits. This stage will probably be handled by your contractor, but it's crucial to make sure the site is properly prepped to prevent problems later in the building process.

EXCAVATION: In accordance with the details of your design plan, the contractor will dig a hole to the required depth and form. Excavated dirt can either be hauled away from the site or utilized for landscaping or backfilling later on in the project.

INSTALL **the pool or spa structure:** The installation of the structure will differ depending on the kind and material of your pool or spa. In order to make the pool shell for concrete pools, the contractor excavates a steel rebar structure inside the hole, then pours gunite or shotcrete over it. While fiberglass pools require the insertion of a prefabricated shell into the dug pit, vinyl liner pools include the installation of prefabricated wall panels and a custom-fit liner.

INSTALL **the plumbing and electrical systems:** After the pool or spa construction is in place, the plumbing and electrical systems need to be installed. For water circulation, filtration, heating, and any other features like waterfalls or jets, this also includes running pipes and conduits. To guarantee safety and adherence to local standards, a certified electrician should install electrical components such as lighting and control systems.

. . .

INSTALL THE COPING AND DECKING: The coping, which is the material used to crown the edge of the pool or spa, gives the area a completed appearance and a seamless transition to the next deck. Precast concrete, brick, and natural stone can all be used as coping materials. Your pool or spa's decking should be made of sturdy, nonslip materials that go in with the overall landscape and decor.

INSTALL the pool or spa equipment: Your contractor will put in the pumps, filters, heaters, and sanitizing systems that are required for your pool or spa. For optimum performance and efficiency, make sure the equipment is properly sized and installed in accordance with the manufacturer's instructions.

INSTALL SAFETY FEATURES: It is crucial to include safety elements in the design of your pool or spa, as was covered in the previous chapter. As part of this, fences or barriers with self-closing gates and alarms, as well as handrails and non-slip surfaces, must be installed. For details on particular safety standards, see your local construction rules and regulations.

· · ·

ONCE THE BUILDING IS FINISHED, you may fill and balance the water in your pool or spa. The water chemistry should be tested and balanced by your contractor in accordance with industry norms and manufacturer guidelines. Maintaining the health and clarity of your pool or spa's water as well as safeguarding the machinery and surfaces from harm depends on proper water balance.

CONDUCT a final inspection and walkthrough with your contractor before utilizing your new pool or spa to be sure that all areas of the project were finished to your satisfaction. This is a chance to discuss any problems or concerns, as well as go through how to use and maintain the spa or pool's equipment.

LANDSCAPING AND FINAL TOUCHES: Now that the pool or spa construction is complete, you can concentrate on the landscaping and finishing touches to make your outdoor space seem put together and welcoming. To improve your pool or spa experience, you may do things like plant trees, bushes, and flowers, put in outside lighting, and add chairs or other amenities.

· · ·

YOU CAN GUARANTEE a successful pool or spa installation that fulfills your needs and expectations by adhering to these procedures and working closely with a reliable contractor. Always put safety and adherence to regional standards and laws first, and contact experts as needed throughout the process. Once your pool or spa is set up and ready to use, you can take advantage of all the advantages it has to offer, from entertainment and relaxation to higher property values and better quality of life.

pool and spa maintenance and troubleshooting

. . .

THE LONG-TERM HEALTH and safety of your pool or spa depend on proper maintenance and prompt troubleshooting. Maintaining the water quality and extending the life of your pool or spa equipment can help keep you and your visitors safe and happy. We will go over important maintenance procedures and typical problem-solving advice in this chapter for your pool or spa.

Maintenance

VACUUMING AND SKIMMING: To get rid of leaves, dirt, and insects, skim the surface of your pool or spa on a regular basis. To get rid of accumulated dirt, sand, and other debris, vacuum the pool or spa floor. By doing this, you can preserve water quality and lessen the strain on your filtration system.

CLEANING THE FILTER: Follow the manufacturer's instructions for cleaning or replacing the filter media, depending on the kind of filter you have (sand, cartridge, or diatomaceous earth). A clean filter will increase water flow and filtration effectiveness, resulting in cleaner water and less need for chemical additives.

MONITORING WATER CHEMISTRY: Perform regular pH, alkalinity, sanitizer, and other tests on the water in your spa or pool as directed by the manufacturer. To maintain the right balance and avoid problems like algae development, discoloration, and damage to equipment or surfaces, adjust the water's chemistry as necessary.

TREATMENT WITH SHOCK: Apply periodic shocks to the water in your pool or spa to get rid of pollutants and keep the water clear. Based on the size and usage of your pool or spa, follow the manufacturer's recommendations for the right kind and quantity of shock treatment.

EQUIPMENT INSPECTION: Check your pool or spa's pumps, filters, heaters, and sanitizing systems frequently for wear or damage. If necessary, replace or fix any broken parts to preserve maximum effectiveness and efficiency.

Troubleshooting

CLOUDY WATER: Unbalanced water chemistry, poor filtration, or the presence of algae can all lead to cloudy water. Check and correct the chemistry of your water, clean or replace the filter media, and make sure the circulation system is operating properly. If the problem continues, think about employing a flocculant or clarifier to assist the water become cleaner.

. . .

ALGAE DEVELOPMENT: Low sanitizer levels, poor water circulation, or unbalanced water chemistry can all lead to the formation of algae in your pool or spa. Shock your pool or spa, brush the impacted areas, and vacuum any debris to cure algae. To stop the formation of algae in the future, modify the chemistry of your water, check your sanitizer levels, and make sure your circulation system is working properly.

STAINS AND SCALING: When minerals, metals, or organic substances accumulate on your pool or spa surfaces, stains and scaling may result. Use a stain and scale remover as directed by the manufacturer to get rid of stains and scaling by balancing the chemistry of your water. By routinely testing and changing your water chemistry, you may stop future scaling and discoloration.

LEAKS: Your pool or spa equipment, plumbing, or building may have leaks. Check your plumbing and equipment for leaks by looking for moist areas in your yard or water pools around the equipment pad. Consult a professional to inspect and fix the problem if you think there may be a leak in your pool or spa construction.

. . .

EQUIPMENT MALFUNCTIONS: If the equipment in your pool or spa isn't working correctly, look for any visible problems first, including obstructions in the pump or filter, loose or broken cabling, or tripped circuit breakers. If the problem continues, go to the manufacturer's troubleshooting manual or get help from a specialist.

YOUR POOL or spa will last longer and operate more effectively if you do routine maintenance and take care of minor problems right away. If you are confused about how to maintain or troubleshoot your pool or spa or if you need help making modifications for maximum operation, always seek expert advice.

exploring other water features: fountains and ponds

. . .

OTHER WATER ELEMENTS, such as fountains and ponds, can improve the beauty and tranquility of your outdoor space in addition to pools and spas. These elements may serve as a focal point in your landscape design, induce a calming atmosphere, and draw animals. The advantages, design factors, and maintenance advice for fountains and ponds will all be covered in this chapter.

Benefits of Ponds and Fountains

AESTHETIC APPEAL: Fountains and ponds enhance your landscape's aesthetic appeal by adding visual interest and beauty. They also serve as a focal point that attracts attention and harmonizes with the surroundings.

CALMING: A soothing environment is created by the sound of running water from a fountain or the softly moving water in a pond, which encourages relaxation and stress reduction.

WILDLIFE ATTRACTION: Fountains and ponds may both draw birds and other wildlife to your outdoor space, while ponds can provide a habitat for fish, frogs, and other aquatic animals.

INCREASED PROPERTY VALUE: Water features that are well-designed and kept up may raise the charm and value of your home overall.

Considerations for Design

STYLE AND MATERIALS: Pick a fountain or pond style and materials that go well with your landscape and architectural architecture. Fountains can be made of materials including stone, concrete, metal, or glass and can have designs that range from minimalist to elaborately classical. Pond designs might be more formal and geometric or more realistic and organic.

SIZE AND PLACEMENT: Take into account the fountain or pond's size and location in relation to the available area and other landscaping features. Make sure the feature can be seen and reached from important outside spaces, including patios, decks, or lounging places.

WATER FILTRATION AND CIRCULATION: Maintaining the health and clarity of your fountain or pond requires effective water filtration and circulation. Include a filtering system to get dirt and impurities out of the water as well as a pump to move it around.

LIGHTS: Include lights in the design of your fountain or pond to improve its aesthetic appeal and produce an enthralling display at night. Submerged lights, spotlights, and accent lights are available to brighten the surrounding environment and the water.

Tips for Maintenance

REGULAR MAINTENANCE: To get rid of dirt, algae, and mineral buildup, periodically clean your fountain or pond. In addition to cleaning the pump and filter parts, this may entail draining and scouring the fountain basin or pond liner.

WATER CHEMISTRY: To maintain a favorable habitat for fish and plants, keep an eye on your pond's water chemistry and make any adjustments. Test your pond's pH, ammonia, nitrite, and nitrate levels, and make any necessary adjustments based on the advice given for the ecology of your particular pond.

PLANT MAINTENANCE: If your pond has aquatic plants, trim any dead or overgrown foliage frequently and get rid of any invasive species that can harm the ecology.

. . .

WILDLIFE PROTECTION: Provide hiding spots, such submerged boulders or aquatic vegetation, and use deterrents, like netting or decoys, to keep predators like raccoons or herons away from your pond and its residents.

WINTER MAINTENANCE: In colder climes, drain or cover your fountain or pond and add a pond heater or de-icer to avoid freezing and safeguard fish and plants.

YOU MAY CONSTRUCT a beautiful and useful fountain or pond that enriches your outdoor area and offers countless hours of enjoyment by taking these design and maintenance considerations into account. To guarantee the success and endurance of your water feature, consult with experts as needed during the design, installation, and maintenance phases.

installing and maintaining fountains

. . .

FOUNTAINS MAY BRING aesthetic appeal and a calming atmosphere to your environment, making them a compelling feature. Your fountain will last a long time and function at its best if it is installed and maintained correctly. The crucial procedures for setting up and maintaining a fountain in your outdoor area will be covered in this chapter.

Setting Up a Fountain

PICK THE IDEAL FOUNTAIN: Opt for a fountain that fits within your available area and matches your landscape and architectural architecture. Think about things like the fountain's design, construction, size, and water flow.

DECIDE ON A GOOD LOCATION: Pick a spot for your fountain that can be seen and reached from important outside spaces, including patios, decks, or lounging areas. Make sure the ground is sturdy and level, and take into account things like wind direction, sun exposure, and the distance to electrical outlets.

SET UP THE LOCATION: Remove any rubbish, rocks, or obstructions from the area where your fountain will be situated before clearing and leveling it. You might need to build a sturdy base using concrete or compacted gravel depending on the size and weight of your fountain to provide stability and support.

FOLLOW the manufacturer's directions for building and installing your fountain while putting it together. This may entail joining the different parts, including the basin, tiers, and ornamental accents, as well as fastening the pump and water circulation tubing.

. . .

CONNECT THE ELECTRICAL COMPONENTS: Make sure the pump and any lighting components are connected to an outside electrical outlet specifically designated for outdoor use with a ground fault circuit interrupter (GFCI). If you are uncertain about any element of the electrical installation, speak with a certified electrician.

FILL THE FOUNTAIN WITH WATER: Pour water into the fountain basin, making sure the pump is completely immersed. To get the proper flow and sound from your fountain, adjust the water level as necessary.

Upkeep of a Fountain

MAINTAIN the fountain by periodically draining it and cleaning it to get rid of dirt, algae, and mineral buildup. With a gentle brush and light detergent, clean the basin, tiers, and ornamental components, being careful not to harm the fountain's materials or finish.

To ENSURE appropriate water circulation and avoid blockage, regularly clean the pump and filter components of the fountain. For detailed cleaning and maintenance requirements, refer to the manufacturer's instructions.

CHECKING the water level in your fountain on a regular basis can help to guarantee that the pump is always completely immersed. The pump may overheat or suffer other harm as a result of low water levels.

AVOID FREEZING YOUR FOUNTAIN: In colder areas, take precautions to avoid freezing your fountain over the winter. After draining the fountain, keep the pump and any other removable parts inside. If at all feasible, move smaller fountains indoors or cover the fountain with a weather-resistant cover.

CHECK for damage to the fountain: Check your fountain often for indications of deterioration, such as cracks, chips, or leaks. In order to stop further degradation and keep the fountain operating at its peak capacity, any damaged components should be repaired or replaced right away.

. . .

YOU CAN PROLONG the life and beauty of your fountain, ensuring countless hours of enjoyment and a fascinating focal point in your outdoor area, by according to these installation and maintenance instructions. To guarantee the success and durability of your fountain, get expert advice when needed for assistance with installation, maintenance, or repairs.

designing and building garden ponds

. . .

WITH A HABITAT for aquatic life and animals as well as a calming focal point for your landscape design, garden ponds may turn your outdoor area into a serene haven. To ensure the success and durability of a garden pond, meticulous planning, execution, and continuous upkeep are necessary. In this chapter, we'll go through the necessary stages for planning and constructing a garden pond, as well as some advice and best practices to keep in mind along the way.

ESTABLISH **the function and design of your pond:** Consider your garden pond's principal function and preferred aesthetic before you begin creating it. Will it be a formal koi pond, a straightforward, naturalistic water element, or a combination of the two? The function and aesthetic of your pond will affect its placement, size, and material selection.

DECIDE ON A GOOD LOCATION: Pick a spot for your pond that can be seen and reached from important outside spaces, including patios, decks, or lounging places. Make sure the ground is level and solid, and take into account variables like sun exposure, wind direction, and distance from trees or other landscape features that may have an influence on the health and upkeep of your pond.

PLAN THE POND'S DIMENSIONS, contours, and depth: Plan your pond's size, shape, and depth after choosing a location. You should take into account the available area, the kinds and numbers of aquatic animals and vegetation, as well as any potential municipal laws or limits. Uneven forms with different depths may give a pond a more organic appearance for a naturalistic setting. Geometric designs and constant depths could be more suited for a formal pond.

· · ·

CHOOSE your pond liner and building supplies:
Choose a pond liner that is strong, flexible, and UV
and puncture-resistant. Materials like reinforced polyethylene, PVC, or EPDM rubber can be used to make
pond liners. You may also think about premade fiberglass or hard plastic pond shells for a more solid pond
building. Additionally, use natural stone, brick, or wood
for the pond's edge so that it blends in with your architectural style and surroundings.

**PLAN THE FILTRATION and circulation systems for
your pond:** To maintain water quality and clarity, a
well-functioning pond needs sufficient filtration and
circulation. Include a filtering system to get dirt and
impurities out of the water as well as a pump to move
it around. A skimmer and an aerator may also be
included in your design to aid with surface particle
removal and water oxygenation, respectively.

**PLAN THE LANDSCAPE and surroundings around
your pond:** Take into account the plants, rocks, and
other components that will encircle and improve your
pond. To build a healthy and diversified environment,
consider include a range of aquatic plants, such as
submerged plants, floating plants, and marginal plants.

Include rocks, driftwood, and other organic materials to give fish and other creatures visual appeal and cover.

PREPARE the pond location by excavating it: Make sure the walls are sturdy and the bottom is level as you carefully excavate the pond area in accordance with your intended design. Take out any sharp pebbles or other anything that can hurt the pond liner. Build a sturdy foundation if required for the pond's edge or any integrated features, such as retaining walls or waterfalls.

INSTALL the edging and pond liner: To guard against punctures, lay down a layer of protective underlayment, such as sand or geotextile cloth. Install the pond liner next, making sure to gently shape it to the size and curves of the pond. Trim any extra liner as necessary after securing it with the edging materials, such as stones or bricks.

SET up the filtration and circulation systems for the pond: Installing the pump, filtration system, skimmer, and aerator for your pond should be done in accordance with the manufacturer's recommendations.

Make that the electrical components are connected to an outside electrical outlet that is specifically designated and equipped with a ground fault circuit interrupter (GFCI). If you are uncertain about any element of the electrical installation, speak with a certified electrician.

FILL YOUR POND WITH WATER, making sure it covers any submerged equipment and gives enough depth for aquatic plants and animals. Next, add plants and fauna. Introduce a variety of aquatic plants in accordance with your design, and when the pond's ecology has had some time to develop, think about adding fish or other pond creatures like snails or frogs.

FINISHING TOUCHES AND LANDSCAPING: Complete the landscaping surrounding your pond by including any extra plants, pebbles, or other ornamental components that you had in mind. To improve the aesthetics of your pond at night, you could also wish to add illumination, such submerged or accent lights.

MAINTAINING your garden pond regularly will ensure its success and long-term health. This maintenance should include checking the water's chemistry, cleaning the pond and filtration system, trimming and removing dead or overgrown plants, and safeguarding your pond from predators and bad weather.

YOU MAY MAKE a beautiful and useful water feature that beautifies your outdoor space and offers countless hours of enjoyment by following these instructions and carefully considering the design, installation, and maintenance elements of your garden pond. To guarantee the success and durability of your pond, consult experts as needed during the design, installation, and maintenance phases.

pond maintenance and troubleshooting

. . .

IN ADDITION to being aesthetically pleasing, a well-kept backyard pond maintains a thriving ecology for wildlife and plants. For your pond to last a long time and to avoid frequent problems, regular care is crucial. In this chapter, we'll go through important pond upkeep chores and troubleshooting advice for typical pond issues.

Maintenance of ponds

To GUARANTEE a healthy habitat for fish and plants, regularly check the pH, ammonia, nitrite, and nitrate levels in your pond's water. In order to maintain the appropriate balance for your particular pond environment, adjust the water chemistry as necessary with pond treatments or water conditioners.

POND AND FILTRATION SYSTEM CLEANING: Regularly clean your pond by removing debris like leaves and twigs that can build up and affect the water's quality. To maintain appropriate water circulation and avoid clogs, clean your pond's pump, filtration system, and skimmer. You may need to partially or completely empty the pond for comprehensive cleaning, depending on its size and design.

MAINTAIN: Trim aquatic plants on a regular basis to prevent overcrowding and remove any dead or rotting foliage that may be causing the water to become contaminated. Keep an eye out for invasive plant species that can harm the pond's environment and get rid of them right once.

DEFEND your pond from predators so that it may remain inhabited: Give fish and other pond dwellers somewhere to hide, such submerged boulders or aquatic vegetation, and use deterrents like netting or fake prey to keep predators like herons or raccoons away.

PLAN AHEAD: Prepare your pond for winter by removing any sensitive plants, adding a pond heater or de-icer to avoid freezing, and ensuring adequate aeration in colder locations. If you have fish, make sure they have access to ample oxygen and space to swim about in the pond's deeper sections.

How to Fix Common Pond Issues

GREEN WATER OR ALGAE BLOOMS: An imbalance in nutrients, sunshine, and water chemistry can result in excessive algae development. Reduce the quantity of sunlight that enters your pond by adding floating plants, such water lilies, or by applying pond dye to fight algae. Maintain adequate water filtration and chemistry, and think about introducing helpful microorganisms to aid in the breakdown of organic waste.

. . .

CLOUDY OR MURKY WATER: Insufficient filtration, an imbalance in the water's chemistry, or suspended particles in the water can all contribute to poor water clarity. Make sure the filtration system in your pond is working properly and keep it clean. In order to help settle suspended particles, consider employing a pond clarifier and modifying the water's chemistry as necessary.

FISH HEALTH PROBLEMS: Lethargy, loss of appetite, or unusual behavior are symptoms of stress or disease in fish. Maintain a close eye on the water chemistry and temperature in your pond, and provide your fish a food that is well-balanced. If you believe your fish may be suffering from a specific disease or parasite, speak with a pond expert or veterinarian.

LEAKS OR WATER LOSS: If the water level in your pond has significantly dropped, there may be a leak in the pond liner or the piping. Examine your pond for leaks by looking for moist patches along the edge or odd pools of water. If necessary, fix or replace the plumbing parts or the pond liner.

. . .

PROBLEMS with the pump or filtration system: If the pump or filtration system in your pond is not working properly, look for obstructions or debris accumulation that may be preventing water flow. Make that the pump is powered by a dedicated GFCI-protected outlet and is completely submerged. For assistance in diagnosing a specific problem, speak with a pond expert or refer to the manufacturer's instructions.

YOU CAN KEEP a pond ecology healthy, beautiful, and thriving by doing routine pond care and addressing possible issues right away. To maintain the success and durability of your garden pond, consult with pond specialists as needed for assistance with upkeep, troubleshooting, or repairs. Your pond will be a calming and alluring center point in your outdoor area for many years to come with the right upkeep and maintenance.

conclusion

· · ·

WE HAVE DELVED into the design, installation, and maintenance of a variety of water features, including sprinklers, pools, spas, fountains, and garden ponds throughout this book, revealing the fascinating world of outdoor plumbing projects. You can turn your outdoor area into a useful, lovely, and sustainable sanctuary that offers you and your family countless hours of enjoyment by learning the concepts, procedures, and best practices for each sort of water feature.

IT IS crucial to approach each project with careful planning, attention to detail, and a commitment to ongoing maintenance, regardless of whether you have chosen to install a practical sprinkler system to keep your lawn and garden lush and green or opted for the tranquil beauty of a garden pond teeming with aquatic life. This helps avert possible problems and pricey future maintenance while also ensuring the performance and durability of your water feature.

EVERY SUCCESSFUL OUTDOOR plumbing project is built on appropriate planning and design, as we have covered throughout this book. Before starting your water feature project, think about things like the area you have available, your budget, and the aesthetic you want. Make sure your project complies with regional laws, safety requirements, and industry best practices by doing in-depth research and consulting experts as necessary.

WHETHER YOU DECIDE to do the job yourself or seek expert assistance, having a sound strategy in place will allow you to move forward with the installation procedure in confidence. Every stage of the installation procedure, from preparing the ground for your sprinkler system to building the ideal pool or spa, calls for dexterity, expertise, and adherence to the manufacturer's instructions and industry standards. You can assure the best performance and lifespan of your water feature by taking the time to carry out each stage correctly.

ANY OUTDOOR WATER feature must undergo regular care in order to maintain both its aesthetic appeal and practical viability, as well as the ecosystem it is a part of. Regular maintenance tasks are necessary for preventing common problems and guaranteeing the long-term success of your water feature, whether you are adjusting your sprinkler system for seasonal changes, cleaning your pool or spa to maintain water quality, or caring for the delicate balance of your garden pond.

WE HAVE DISCUSSED the visual components that add to the overall attractiveness and enjoyment of your outdoor water feature in addition to the practical issues of design, installation, and upkeep. You may construct a unified and alluring outdoor area that reflects your own taste and vision by carefully choosing materials, plants, and decorative accents that go with your land-scape and architectural design.

· · ·

REMEMBER that each water feature is distinct and may call for a tailored strategy to design, installation, and upkeep as you set out on your outdoor plumbing project adventure. Be ready to change and learn as you go, asking for advice from experts and other enthusiasts to improve your tactics and get around obstacles as necessary.

IN CONCLUSION, there are countless options for creativity, self-expression, and a connection to the natural world in the area of outdoor plumbing projects. You can create an outdoor place that not only improves the beauty and value of your home but also adds joy, relaxation, and inspiration to your everyday life by taking the time to carefully plan, design, install, and manage your water feature. So enjoy the procedure, the long-lasting benefits, and the experience of creating your very own outdoor water feature.

If you enjoyed this book please leave a review so others can find it and benefit they way we hope you have!

MORE PLUMBING RESOURCES
BY HARPER WELLS

PLUMBING BOOK FOR BEGINNERS
BOOK 1

PEX PIPE PLUMBING FOR BEGINNERS
BOOK 2

**ADVANCED PLUMBING TECHNIQUES
BOOK 3**

**WATER HEATER MASTERY
BOOK 4**

**ECO-FRIENDLY PLUMBING SOLUTIONS
BOOK 5**

FREEBOOKDAILY.COM

Made in the USA
Las Vegas, NV
20 September 2024